The LUCKIEST CHILD
Becoming a Blended Family

Written By Zoie Seay

Imprint of The Moose Express, LLC

THE MOOSE EXPRESS

hop on the book train

Printed in the United States of America
Library of Congress Number: 2021920725
ISBN: 978-1-7379583-0-7
www.themooseexpressbooks.com

Dedication

To the love of my life, Zack, who has believed in me every step of the way;
to Brytnii, the mother of my stepson; and to Jaxon,
who made me the luckiest stepmom and gave me the courage
and motivation to write this book.
Also, to my parents, who have always been my biggest fans and
supporters. Lastly, to the Warrior Stepmoms who have
helped me and to anyone who belongs to a blended family.

What does it mean to be part of a blended family?

Being part of a blended family may simply mean that you have an extra parent, like a stepmom or stepdad, who loves you. But not all blended families look the same. Being part of a blended family may mean different things, depending on the experience. Together we can find out what it means to you.

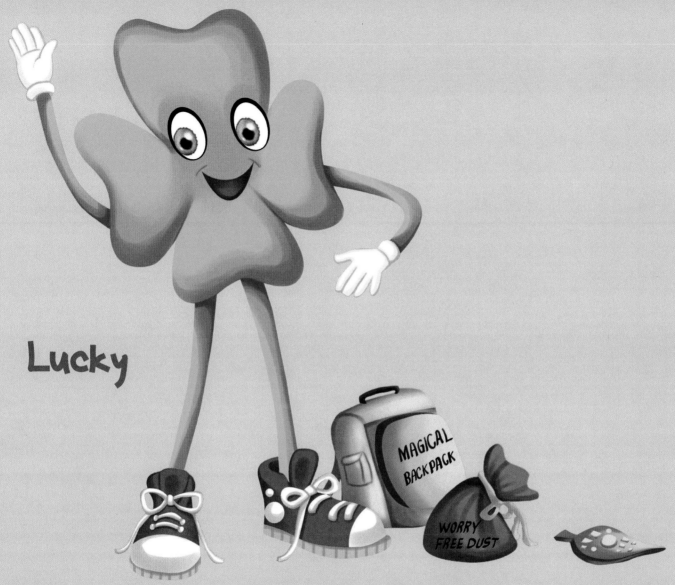

Lucky

Lucky is a magical Four-Leaf Clover that only children can see. He helps children understand what it means to belong to a blended family. He also has magical powers, magical worry-free dust, Leaf TV Remote, a shoe that is used as a time machine, and a special backpack with other magical tools.

Have you ever felt as if your whole world is topsy-turvy?
Are you afraid of the new changes happening in your life, and you
don't know if you should embrace them or run and scream?
Well, that's exactly how I felt, and I didn't know what to do.

Here's My Story

My name is Little Bear, and I have so many questions bouncing up and down inside my head like a trampoline!

The other night, during dinner, my Papa Bear said, "Son, I have some wonderful news to share with you. Guess who's coming to live with us!"

"Hmmmm... I know! Grandma and Grandpa Bear," I exclaimed. The thought of them coming to live with us made me happy and excited because it's always so much fun whenever they visit.

"No, silly Bear," said Papa. "Guess again!"

9

"I know, I know! It's Mama Bear!"
"No, Buddy," said Papa Bear. "Your mama and I live in separate homes, and that won't change, but neither will our love for you."

"Oh, shucks. Okay, well, I give up. Tell me! Tell me!"
"It's Ruby! We're getting married. You, Ruby, and I are going to be a Blended Family," said Papa.
Huh? Wait! What?

11

Suddenly I felt confused, sad, and very nervous. I didn't know what a Blended Family was. Even though I want Papa Bear to be happy, I wasn't sure if I liked the idea of him getting married or Ruby coming to live with us. After all, it's been just us boys for quite sometime.

Papa Bear explained that a Blended Family is when two grown ups come together and one or both have children from a previous relationship. He told me that when they get married, Ruby will be my Step-mama Bear. "Step-mama" or "Step-papa" are parents who aren't your birth Mama or Papa Bear.

I immediately thought, *What about Mama Bear?*

Oh no. It seemed like everything was going to change, and I didn't like that feeling.

That night I went to bed feeling anxious and sad. I really like Ruby, but I had so many questions.

15

The very next day, while sitting in my backyard, I heard a strange voice. "Hi! Are you okay? You look sad."

The voice belonged to a four-leaf clover! I was so shocked, I couldn't even answer.

How crazy is this? An actual talking four-leaf clover is in my backyard. And look at those shoes!

"My name is Lucky, and I'm a magical four-leaf clover. What's your name?" he asked.

"Uh, my name is Little Bear," I answered shyly. "Where did you come from, and what do you mean, *magical*?"

18

"I came to you from a faraway land, and I'm on a special mission to help you," Lucky said proudly.

"My job is to help children understand how belonging to a Blended Family can be a gift.

I use magical tools to help me do that, and oh—I almost forgot. Only *you* can see me!"

"Wow, really?" I asked. "That's super awesome! This is great because I have so many questions. Yesterday, my Papa Bear told me that he and Ruby are getting married and that we will become a Blended Family. "But what if Papa Bear doesn't spend as much time with me anymore?

Or what if he only wants to spend time with Ruby? Oh no, I'm doooomed, "I wailed, burying my face in my paws. "Don't worry, Little Bear. We will get through this together," said Lucky as he took off one of his shoes.

"Let's take a magical journey back in time to the day you were born. I have something to show you that will help calm all those jitterbugs you're feeling inside."

With the quick press of a button on the inside of Lucky's shoe, we flashed back in time.

"On the day you were born, your Mama and Papa Bear became the luckiest parents. You were a gift that filled their hearts with the strongest love. Together, your parents did their best to care for you and show you love every day. Do you see how happy and loved you are?" asked Lucky.

"I sure do," I answered.

"But, as you grew older, Mama and Papa Bear had to make a hard decision, which was to live in separate homes. This was so they could be the best they could be to best raise you. And to this day, their love for you hasn't faded—not one teensy-tiny little bit," Lucky explained. *Wow!* That made me feel all warm and cozy inside...and proud too.

"So, always remember that no matter who joins your family, no one can ever change the special connection you have with your Mama and Papa Bear—not even Ruby Bear.

"And no way would Papa Bear miss the chance to rough house, play games, and build new inventions with you, just like the good ol' days.

In fact, you might even get to do even *more* fun things because Ruby Bear may have some exciting ideas of her own."
"You're right, Lucky!" I said, remembering how creative and fun Ruby Bear is.

"What are you looking for, Lucky?" I asked as he rummaged through his backpack.

"I'm looking for my magical Leaf TV Remote," Lucky said. "Aha, I found it! I'm ready for your next question."

"Oh! Well, what if Ruby Bear and Mama Bear don't get along, like me and my friend Jackson Bear?" I asked. Sometimes Jackson and I fight about silly things, like who gets to go down the slide first or which game we are going to play next.

"Well, guess what—grown ups have disagreements too, but that doesn't mean that they can't work it out. Learning to get along is a part of life, even after you are grown up.

Do you and Jackson Bear stay mad at each other whenever you disagree? Or do you talk it through and try to make things better?" Lucky asked.

"We never stay mad very long. We usually are able to talk it out."

"Well, that's what grownups do!"

"Thanks, Lucky! I'm starting to feel so much better. Will you come visit me tomorrow?"

"Of course!" said Lucky. "I'll meet you right here by the swing."

The very next morning, I jumped out of bed so early that it was still a little dark out.

Seeing my magical new friend Lucky again made me want to explode with excitement. Before I fell asleep the night before, more questions popped in my head. So, I rushed to brush my chompers, gobbled up my breakfast, and zoomed out the back door to meet Lucky at the tire swing.

"Good morning, Little Bear," Lucky said as soon as he appeared.

"Good morning, Lucky,"I gasped, out of breath from rushing.

"So, what shall we chat about today?" he asked.

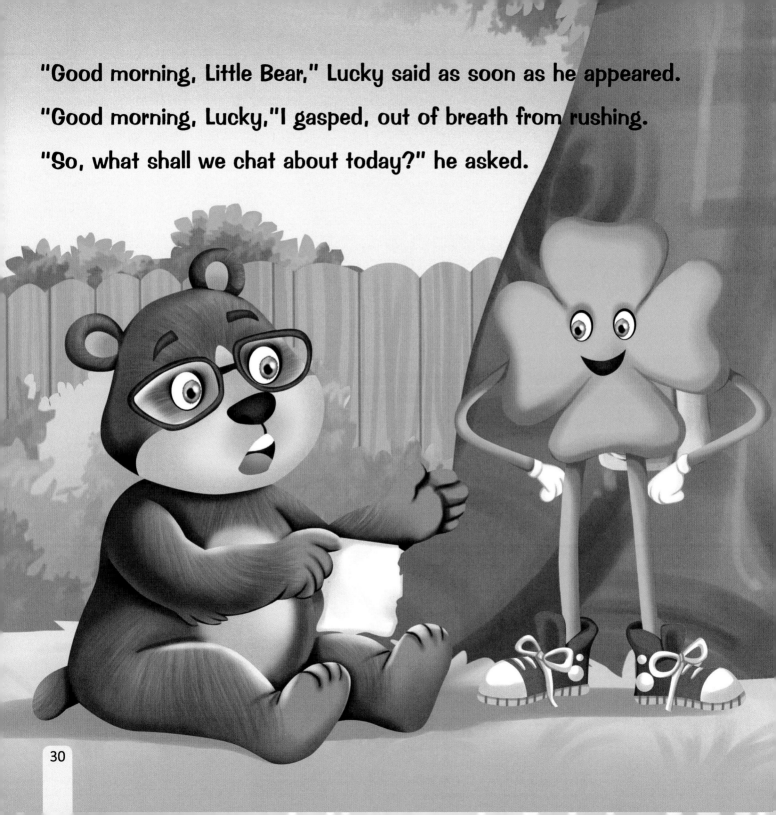

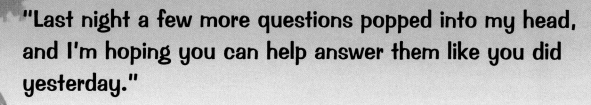

"Last night a few more questions popped into my head, and I'm hoping you can help answer them like you did yesterday."

"Absolutely! Let 'er rip," Lucky laughed.

"Well, what if Ruby starts to tell me what to do?" I asked. "Having a new step parent can mean a lot of changes, but that doesn't mean they're bad changes. Always remember, when grown ups tell you what to do, it's because they care about your safety and want what's best for you."

"Yeah, but what if Ruby Bear tries to make a bunch of new rules?" I asked in a wary voice.

"That's a great question," Lucky said as he sprinkled magic dust over my head. "Rules are important because they let you know what is expected of you. They help you to make healthy choices, and they teach you self-control. These are all great tools you will use when you become a grownup."

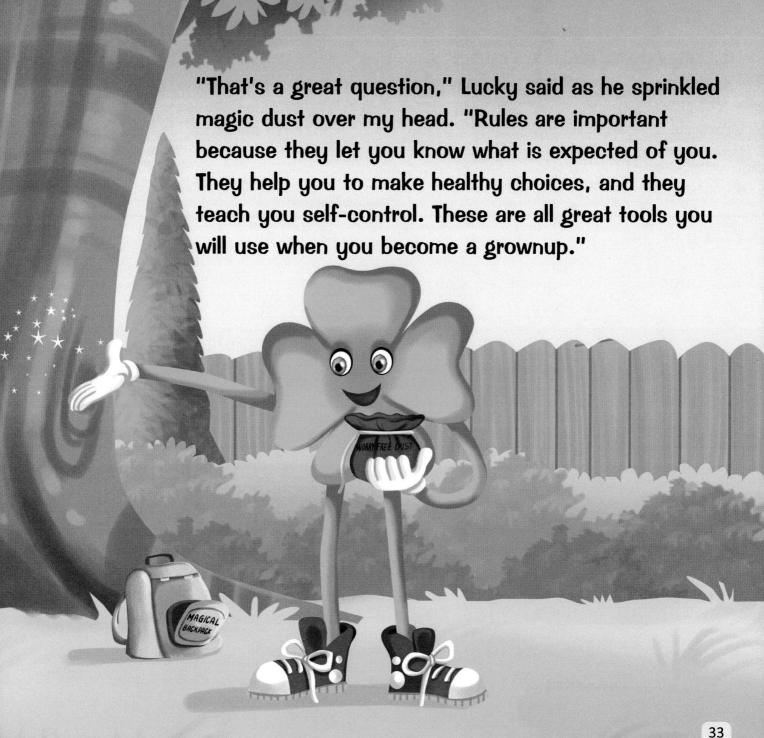

I felt the magic dust settle over me, taking my worries away.
Lucky continued, "No matter if you're at Mama Bear's or
Papa Bear's house, it's important
that you respect the rules and
the grownup who makes
them, including Ruby Bear."

R.E.A.D

R - Respect Others

E - Express Feelings

A - Ask Questions

D - Discuss Concerns

MAGICAL BACKPACK

"But what if I break the rules?" I asked.

"No one expects you to be perfect," Lucky said. "It may be hard at times, but it's always important to do your best to follow the rules. If you don't understand a rule, ask questions. I'm sure Ruby Bear would be happy to explain.

"All your parents want is for you to grow up to be a great leader and someone who makes good choices. That's all Ruby wants as well."

"Lucky, thanks for answering all my questions. I think your mission is complete," I said with a loud chuckle.

"Being in a Blended Family actually sounds way better than I thought. I'm excited to have a step parent who will love me enough to want to create and share memories with me."

Lucky beamed. "I'm happy you're feeling more confident and that you're going to be part of a loving family that works toward raising you to be the best you can be."

"Me too!" I said. "I guess I am pretty lucky!"

6 months Later.......

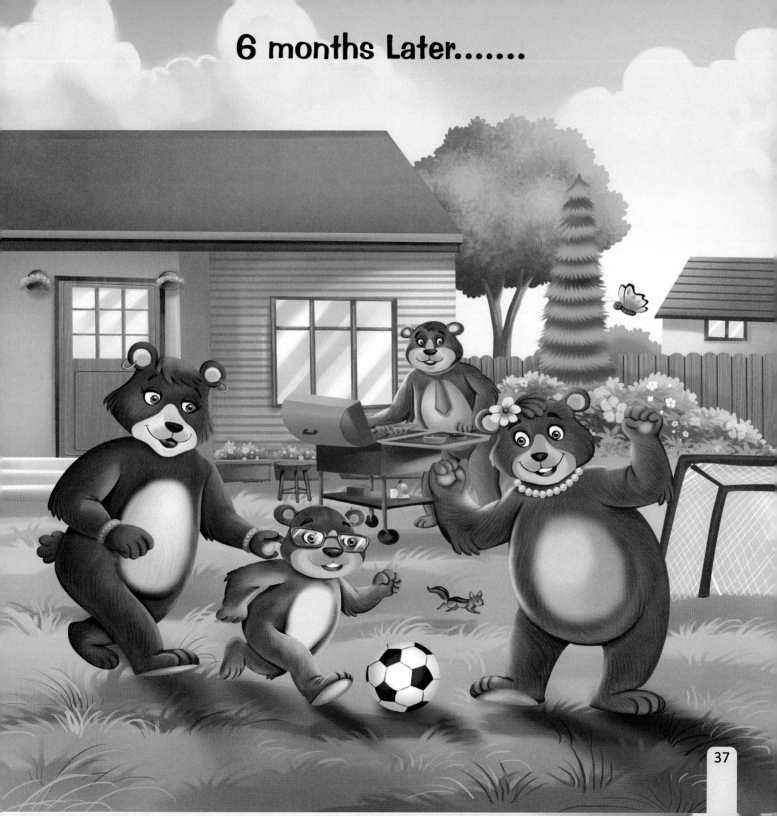

Blended Family Activity

Now that you've learned what a Blended Family is, fill out the information below with your Blended Family.

Blended Family
Photo Here

The_____Family

Est._____

Fill out the information below together.
Each family member writes what being part of a Blended Family means to them.

Name_____

_____

Name_____

_____

Name_____

_____

Name_____

_____

Name_____

_____

What is something the kiddos would like to do as a family?_____

What is something that you have always wanted to say/ask about your Blended Family?

1. _____

2. _____

Here's some important tips and quotes to help you along the way!

"If you're proud, share it out loud!"

- Zoie Seay

"Your voice always matters, but only you can choose to use it."

– Zoie Seay

Changes can be hard, but if you always remember to R.E.A.D., you can handle almost any change.

R – Respect each other
E – Express your feelings
A – Ask Questions
D – Discuss your concerns

Made in the USA
Las Vegas, NV
12 October 2022

57135012R00026